AF172825

My Father's Story

A Family Memory Book

My Father's Story

Polly Chapman

A Family Memory Book

Bedford Square
Publishers

Contents

Jane Austen (1775–1817), *Emma* **(1815)**

'Never could I expect to be so truly beloved and important; so always first and always right in any man's eyes as I am in my father's.'

Dear Dad,

This journal is a way for me to find out more about you; to ask all those questions I forget to ask in the hustle and bustle of everyday life. There are lots of stories I've heard before, the ones that have passed into family history, but I think there is much more that I don't know and would love to learn.

It's not just the big things – where you were born, where you went to school and where you lived as you were growing up – that I'd like to know. I'm also keen to find out about the smaller details of your life. Who were your best friends? When did you first fall in love? How did you discover the hobbies you now spend your time enjoying? All these things will help me to draw up a picture of you, and will perhaps help me to make sense of the way I am.

I'm also really interested to hear about the challenges you faced and how you overcame them, and whether there are any life lessons you feel you can pass on to me.

Thank you so much for taking the time to do this. I'm excited to find out more about your past and hear your reflections on life as my dad.

All dads have different journeys so please just ignore any questions you feel aren't relevant for you.

With all my love,

Cicero (106–43 BC), *Post Reditum ad Populum* (57 BC)

'Of all nature's gifts to the human race, what is sweeter to a man than his children?'

Early Life

Your early years are important in shaping the person you become, so in this section I'd love to hear about your first memories and experiences. What are the fragments and images that float in your head from when you were tiny? Perhaps it's the wallpaper in your bedroom, or a particular toy you loved, or maybe it's an item of clothing?

It would also be wonderful to have a sense of the place where you were brought up – the physical space, your house or flat, perhaps your garden, as well as the people who were around you when you were a child. Who were the figures most important to you at that stage of your life?

I know it's not easy to dig that far back, but perhaps you have photographs that would provide a prompt. If you find a photograph of you, your friends or family from when you were small, please do stick it on the next page.

These early years shaped the man you are today, so please describe as much as you can remember.

....

What are your earliest memories?

_____

_____

_____

_____

_____

_____

_____

Where were you born? Can you describe the home in which you were raised?

_____

_____

_____

_____

_____

_____

_____

What are your strongest memories of the area you were brought up in? Was there a particular park you were taken to? Perhaps there was a sports ground or swimming pool you loved. Was there a corner shop you visited to spend your pocket money? If you did get pocket money, how much did you get?

_____

_____

_____

_____

_____

_____

Did you have a garden? Can you describe it and how you played in it?

_____

_____

_____

_____

_____

_____

What are your earliest memories of your bedroom? Did you have a favourite soft toy? Did you share your bedroom?

_____

_____

_____

_____

_____

_____

Do you remember your neighbours or any babysitters from when you were a child? Who were the most important people in your life, other than your parents?

_____

_____

_____

_____

_____

_____

_____

_____

_____

_____

_____

Are there any birthday parties or other celebrations that particularly stand out? Did you ever have a party entertainer? What games did you play at parties? Feel free to add any photographs here too!

_____

_____

_____

_____

_____

_____

What do you remember about your early years of nursery and school? Can you remember your first day? Was there a 'home corner' or somewhere you loved to be when you were there? What was your favourite thing to play with? Can you remember any of your teachers from nursery?

_____

_____

_____

_____

_____

Were you a naughty child? Can you remember getting into trouble when you were little? What was the worst thing you did?

_____

_____

_____

_____

_____

Were you close to your family? Do you have any photographs of you all together when you were small that you could stick here?

Did you have any pets growing up? If so, what were they called? What did you do to help look after them? If you didn't have a pet, would you have wanted one?

_____

_____

_____

_____

_____

_____

Did you go on family holidays? Which were the holidays you particularly remember?

_____

_____

_____

_____

_____

Did you play games together as a family? What are the games you most enjoyed – are they the same as the ones we played?

_____

_____

_____

_____

_____

_____

What are the family gatherings or parties that you really remember when you were small?

_____

_____

_____

_____

_____

How often did you see your wider family – aunts, uncles and cousins? Are there relatives you saw a lot back then, but who you have lost touch with now?

_____

_____

_____

_____

_____

What was your favourite food when you were young? Was the food you had very different from the food you gave me when I was little?

_____

_____

_____

_____

_____

Fact File
What was your first address?
How long did you live there?
What was the name of your favourite toy?
What was the name of your nursery?
What was the name of your favourite babysitter?
Do you remember the name of your closest friend at nursery?
What was the name of your pet?

William Wordsworth (1770–1850), *Michael* **(1800)**

'A child more than all other gifts
That earth can offer to declining man,
Brings hope with it, and forward-looking thoughts.'

Your Parents

I would love to hear more about my grandparents here. They are part of who you are, and it would be wonderful to know a bit more about them.

It would be interesting to try and work out how much you followed the parenting style of your parents, or the degree to which you wanted to do things differently from them. I know them as my grandparents, but I'm sure they were different as parents – what were they like? Were they strict? Were you close to them? What were their best qualities as parents? Can you tell me about the moments you got into trouble, or the times they were especially proud of you?

I can see traits in myself that I think I have inherited from you: I'd love to know if you think there are elements of your personality that you have inherited from your parents. What are the important ways in which you think you were shaped by your upbringing?

....

Do you have any photographs of your mum you could stick here?

Tell me about your mum, what sort of person was she when you were growing up? Did she change as she got older?

_____

_____

_____

_____

_____

_____

Where had your mum been brought up, what sort of life had she lived?

_____

_____

_____

_____

_____

_____

Did your mum work? If so, what did she do?

_____

_____

_____

_____

_____

_____

What sort of relationship did you have with her? Were you close?
How did your relationship with her change when you became a
dad?

_____

_____

_____

_____

_____

_____

What are the personality traits you inherited from your mum? Are there any hobbies or interests you shared with her that she might have passed on to you?

_____

_____

_____

_____

_____

_____

Were there any moments when you fell out with her?

_____

_____

_____

_____

_____

Do you have a photograph of my grandfather you could stick here?

Tell me about him, what sort of person was he?

_____

_____

_____

_____

_____

_____

Did he work? What did he do?

_____

_____

_____

_____

_____

_____

What was his background and where had he been raised? Do you remember visiting his childhood home?

_____

_____

_____

_____

_____

_____

How close were you to him? Do you have memories of special times spent with him? Did he introduce you to things you still enjoy?

_____

_____

_____

_____

_____

_____

How did your parents meet?

_____

_____

_____

_____

_____

_____

Where did my grandparents live when you were born? Did you live in the same house for all of your childhood or did they move?

_____

_____

_____

_____

_____

_____

Do you think you are most like your mum or your dad? In what ways are you like them? Can you see any aspects of them in me?

_____

_____

_____

_____

_____

How do you think the way you were raised was different from the way you have raised me? Were there things about the way you were brought up that you wanted to make sure you did differently as a parent?

_____

_____

_____

_____

_____

What were the best things your parents did for you?

_____

_____

_____

_____

_____

_____

_____

Would you describe your childhood as happy? Is there anything you would change if you could?

_____

_____

_____

_____

_____

_____

_____

Do you remember your own grandparents? What can you tell me about them? Feel free to add any photographs here.

Fact File
What were the full names of your mother and father?
What are their dates of birth?
What are the full names of your grandparents?
What are their dates of birth?
Where was your mother born?
Where was your father born?

Fact File

How many siblings did your mother have?

What are their names?

How many siblings did your father have?

What are their names?

Write three words for each of your parents that you think sums them up.

William Shakespeare (1564–1616), *Henry VI: Part 3* **(1623)**

'Why, 'tis a happy thing
To be the father unto many sons'

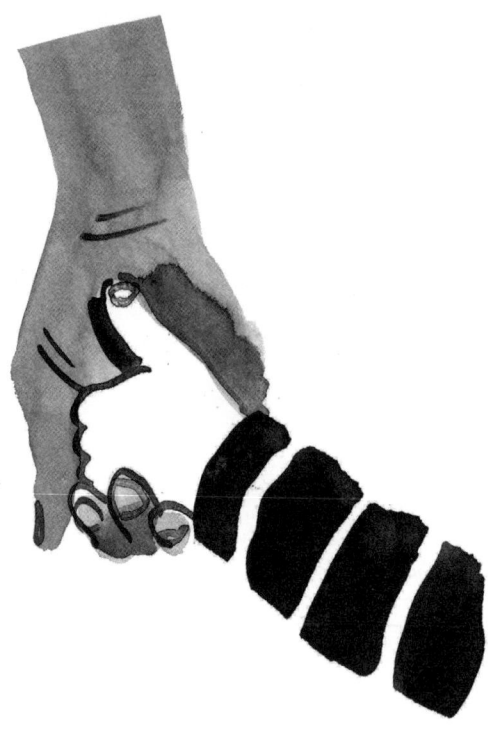

Your School Days

Your years at school are some of the most formative, and I would be really interested to know how you think they made you into the person you are today. It's probably easier to remember your secondary school, but if you can try to think back to primary school, I'd love to know what you found fun or boring – did these things change as you got older? Was there a love of sport that started then? Or of art, drama or reading? What are the overriding memories of your primary school days? Are there any teachers who you were particularly fond of, or who you really didn't like?

I also wonder what you think were the most important aspects of your secondary school education. Was there a teacher who had a profound impact on your future career? Perhaps you first fell in love whilst you were at school, or discovered a work ethic that has stayed with you since. I'd really like to know if you look back on your school days as a happy time – is there anything you would do differently if you could re-live them now?

....

Do you have a photograph of your first day at primary or secondary school that you can stick here?

Where did you go to primary school? Can you remember anything about the buildings? Were you happy there?

_____

_____

_____

_____

_____

_____

What are your strongest memories of primary school? Can you remember the names of any teachers you loved, or any who you really didn't like? Why did you love/dislike them?

_____

_____

_____

_____

_____

_____

Were there any talents you developed at primary school that ended up becoming part of your life now?

_____

_____

_____

_____

_____

_____

Do you remember your friends from primary school? Are you still friends with any of them?

_____

_____

_____

_____

_____

Where did you go to secondary school? Did you enjoy your time there?

_____

_____

_____

_____

_____

_____

What was your favourite subject and why? Was it always your favourite or did you develop a love for it?

_____

_____

_____

_____

_____

_____

Did you have a favourite teacher? Was there someone who inspired you?

_____

_____

_____

_____

_____

_____

Were there any subjects you really couldn't get on with? What were your worst moments in class?

_____

_____

_____

_____

_____

What are your favourite memories from school?

_____

_____

_____

_____

_____

_____

What were the most difficult times you had at school?

_____

_____

_____

_____

_____

_____

What did you enjoy most outside of regular academic lessons?
Was it sport, art, drama, music – what were your favourite extra-curricular activities?

_____

_____

_____

_____

_____

_____

Were there any sports matches, drama productions, concerts or other school events that particularly stick in your mind?

_____

_____

_____

_____

_____

Did you ever get into trouble? If so, what happened and how did your parents react? Did it have any long-term effect on you?

_____

_____

_____

_____

_____

_____

When you think back on your school days, what long-term impact do you think it had on your character?

_____

_____

_____

_____

_____

_____

Was there a particular moment from your school days that stands out as being pivotal to your future life or career?

_____

_____

_____

_____

_____

_____

Can you find any old reports from school that you can photograph and stick here? If not, do you remember anything that they said?

_____

_____

_____

_____

_____

Fact File
What was the name of your secondary school?
What year did you start and when did you leave?
Who was your best friend at secondary school?
What exams did you take and what grades did you get?
What was your worst subject?
What was the name of your head teacher?
What was your most embarrassing moment?

Fact File

What was your proudest moment?

Were you a prefect or in any other position of responsibility?

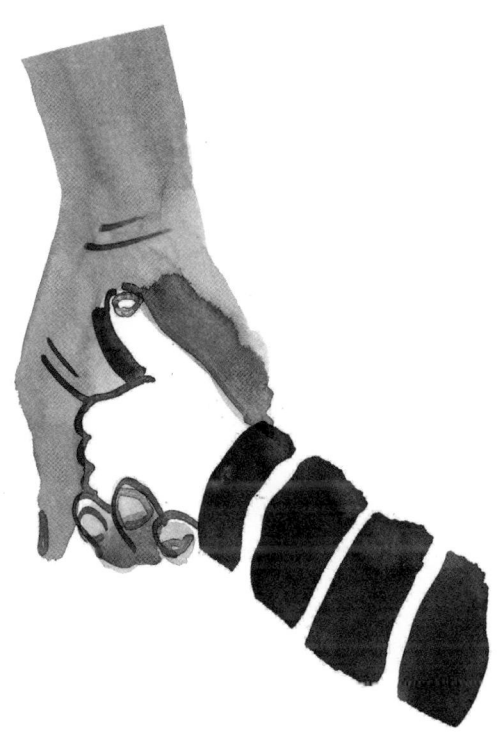

Frances Hodgson Burnett (1849–1924) *A Little Princess* (1905)

'Things happen to people by accident... A lot of nice accidents
have happened to me. It just happened that I always liked lessons
and books, and could remember things when I learned them. It
just happened that I was born with a father who was beautiful
and nice and clever, and could give me everything I liked.'

Being a Teenager

Some of my most vivid memories are from my teenage years. It can be an emotional rollercoaster, a time when we start to figure out who we are and what we believe in. The highs and lows are intense and unforgettable. It can be an exciting but also a confusing time of life and I'm keen to learn how you navigated it.

Do you think it was easier to be a teenager when you were growing up than it was for me? I'm curious to know whether you had the same insecurities and anxieties as I did, or whether we shared any of the same dreams and goals. It's hard for me to imagine you as a teenager, so please do share as much as you feel able to! I'd love to know about the memories that make you smile, or to hear about the challenges you faced.

If you have any photographs of you with some of your friends when you were a teenager, please do stick them in here.

What sort of teenager were you? Did you ever fall out with your parents over things you wanted to do but weren't allowed to?

_____

_____

_____

_____

_____

_____

Who was the person you turned to for advice most often when you were a teenager?

_____

_____

_____

_____

_____

Can you remember your first kiss? Where did it happen and how old were you?

_____

_____

_____

_____

_____

_____

Did you have a first love when you were at school? Who were they and can you describe them?

_____

_____

_____

_____

_____

_____

Did you love music when you were at school? Who were your favourite bands or musicians?

_____

_____

_____

_____

_____

_____

How did you listen to them: radio, records, CDs, cassettes? Did you make mixtapes?

_____

_____

_____

_____

_____

Did you have a favourite book or film when you were a teenager? Was there one that had a profound impact on you?

_____

_____

_____

_____

_____

_____

_____

Did you go to parties when you were a teenager? Did you enjoy them?

_____

_____

_____

_____

_____

_____

Was fashion important to you? Did you care about the clothes you wore? Were there particular styles you loved?

_____

_____

_____

_____

_____

_____

Who were your best friends at the time? What did you all do together? Did you have a favourite place where you would meet up?

_____

_____

_____

_____

_____

Did you have part-time jobs when you were at school? Do you remember how much you were paid?

_____

_____

_____

_____

_____

_____

What were the biggest news stories you remember from your teenage years?

_____

_____

_____

_____

_____

What was the most awkward or embarrassing moment during those years?

_____

_____

_____

_____

_____

_____

Do you have any memories from that time that still make you laugh?

_____

_____

_____

_____

_____

What were your dreams and aspirations? Did you know what you wanted to do for work, or where you wanted to live?

_____

_____

_____

_____

_____

_____

What was the most challenging moment of your teenage years?

_____

_____

_____

_____

_____

_____

If you could wind the clock back and change one thing from that time, what would it be?

_____

_____

_____

_____

_____

_____

What one piece of advice would you give to a young person going through adolescence?

_____

_____

_____

_____

_____

_____

Fact File

Who was your first celebrity crush?

What was the first music concert you went to?

Where did you live when you were a teenager?

What was the name of the place where you most often met up with your friends?

How old were you when you went on holiday with friends for the first time?

Where did you go?

Fact File
What was your favourite TV show?
How did you keep in touch with your friends before mobile phones?

Louisa May Alcott (1832–1888) *Little Women* **(1868)**

'Your father, Jo. He never loses patience, never doubts or complains, but always hopes, and works and waits so cheerfully that one is ashamed to do otherwise before him.'

Life After School

Did you know what you wanted to do when you left school? I would love to know more about the choices you made at this stage, and how long it took you to work out the right path to follow. I wonder if you found it all overwhelming, or whether you always knew what you wanted to do. Were your parents supportive and happy with the decisions you were making? Did you listen to their advice or plough your own furrow?

I'm also interested in how you found the transition from school to work or university. Did you enjoy the freedom, or were there challenges in navigating your way to adulthood? I wonder whether you are happy with the choices you made, or whether there are things you wish you'd done differently?

If you have a photograph of yourself when you left school or started university, or a graduation photograph please stick it here.

What did you do after leaving school? Did you get the grades you needed to move on to the next stage?

_____

_____

_____

_____

_____

_____

Did you go to university? Where did you go and what did you study? If not, did you go straight into work or an apprenticeship?

_____

_____

_____

_____

_____

_____

What were the best and worst things about university or the apprenticeship? Was there a particular moment that was a highlight?

_____

_____

_____

_____

_____

_____

Did you know what you wanted to do for a job or a career? How did you end up in your first job?

_____

_____

_____

_____

_____

Where was your first job? What do you remember about your first day at work?

_____

_____

_____

_____

_____

_____

How quickly did you settle in and how long did you stay in your first job?

_____

_____

_____

_____

_____

_____

What did you like most about the work you were doing?

_____

_____

_____

_____

_____

_____

Did you make good friends at work? Who were they and are you
still in touch with them?

_____

_____

_____

_____

_____

_____

What was the most embarrassing mistake you made when you were at work?

_____

_____

_____

_____

_____

_____

Was there an alternative career you wished you had pursued?

_____

_____

_____

_____

_____

_____

What is the most memorable experience of your working life?

_____

_____

_____

_____

_____

Is there any advice you would give me on how to be happy and successful at work?

_____

_____

_____

_____

_____

Fact File

What was the name of your first boss?

How old were you when you got your first job?

What was your salary when you started work?

What is the most enjoyable job you've ever had?

What was the biggest mistake you made at work?

What was your greatest triumph at work?

Who had the biggest impact on your professional growth?

Laurence Sterne (1713–1768), *The Life and Opinions of Tristram Shandy, Gentleman* (1759)

'I wish either my father or my mother, or indeed both of them, as they were in duty both equally bound to it, had minded what they were about when they begot me.'

Your Friendships

You have lots of friends, some of whom you've known for years. You've shown me through example the importance of good friendship. I'd like to know what qualities you look for in a friend and the ways in which you have been supportive to those close to you.

I'm also interested to hear a little more of the ups and downs of friendship; what you've done when the path hasn't been smooth and the ways in which you've managed to patch things up. Do you have any tips to share?

I have lovely friends now, but I'm interested to learn whether there was a time when you were worried about the friendships I was making. Was there a time when you tried to steer me away from some people, or did you think it better to leave me to find my own path?

....

Who were the first people you remember as being friends at school?

_____

_____

_____

_____

_____

_____

Did they stay good friends? If not, why?

_____

_____

_____

_____

_____

_____

Do you remember a particularly significant falling out of friendship? What happened?

_____

_____

_____

_____

_____

_____

_____

Did you succeed in making up with the friend after the bad falling out? If so, do you remember how you fixed it?

_____

_____

_____

_____

_____

_____

Were you part of one tightly bound friendship group at school, or did you move between different groups?

_____

_____

_____

_____

_____

_____

What do you think drew you to those people?

_____

_____

_____

_____

_____

_____

What are the most important qualities you look for in a friendship? How has this changed over time?

_____

_____

_____

_____

_____

_____

Can you tell me about a couple of moments when close friends have been there for you in difficult times?

_____

_____

_____

_____

_____

_____

What does it take to be a good friend to others? Are there any particular moments when you were able to help a close friend?

_____

_____

_____

_____

_____

_____

What are the funniest, most joyous moments you've shared with friends?

_____

_____

_____

_____

_____

_____

Is there an ideal number of close friends to have?

_____

_____

_____

_____

_____

_____

What do you think of my friends? Were there any moments when you were worried about my friendships and, if so, what did you do about it?

_____

_____

_____

_____

_____

_____

How would your friends describe you?

_____

_____

_____

_____

_____

_____

Would you say you have a best friend now and, if so, who is it and why are they especially important?

_____

_____

_____

_____

_____

_____

Fact File

Who was your first friend?

Who has been your friend for the longest time?

If you had to call a friend in an emergency, who would it be?

Which friend do you laugh the most with?

Is there a friend who you really miss, who you haven't seen in a long time?

Who is your best friend?

Describe your friendship group in three words.

Wilhelm Busch (1832–1908), *Julchen* **(1877)**

'Becoming a father isn't difficult,
But it's very difficult to be a father.'

Becoming a Dad

This section looks at how you felt as you became a dad. It's such a huge life change, and learning more about that moment will help me understand you as a young man rather than just as my dad. I'm interested in how you felt when you found out my mum was pregnant. Was it a surprise? Had you planned it, were you happy, nervous, shocked or a combination of all of them? In pregnancy most of the attention is focused on the mum to be, but I'd love to know about how you felt about the whole thing.

When I arrived, how involved were you in the early stages? Did you stay up at night with me? Did you have much support from your own parents, and did they give you advice? How did you cope with working whilst having disrupted sleep? What did you feel your role was as dad in those first few months? Was it all a shock?

....

If you have a photograph of you holding me just after I was born, please add it here.

When and how did you find out you were going to be a father?

_____

_____

_____

_____

_____

_____

Can you remember exactly how you felt when you found out?

_____

_____

_____

_____

_____

_____

Did you get involved in any ante-natal groups? If so, did you make any good new friends at this stage?

_____

_____

_____

_____

_____

_____

How was my birth? Can you tell me about the day I was born?

_____

_____

_____

_____

_____

_____

What were your first thoughts when you saw me? Did you know in advance whether I was going to be a boy or a girl?

_____

_____

_____

_____

_____

_____

Were you with mum when she went through labour? How did you find the whole experience?

_____

_____

_____

_____

_____

What do you remember most from the early months of my life?
Did you have much help from friends or family?

_____

_____

_____

_____

_____

_____

What sort of baby was I? Was I a good sleeper?

_____

_____

_____

_____

_____

_____

_____

What did you most enjoy, and what were the worst bits of being the father of a young baby?

_____

_____

_____

_____

_____

Was there a particular fashion in parenting when I was young? What was your philosophy in getting through those early years?

_____

_____

_____

_____

_____

Did you read books or look for advice on how to be a good parent? Was there any good advice handed down from parents or in-laws?

_____

_____

_____

_____

_____

_____

What sacrifices did you have to make to be a dad? Was there anything you wish you'd done differently?

_____

_____

_____

_____

_____

Did you manage to keep up with your hobbies and friends at this point? Was there anything you were doing that you had to cut back?

_____

_____

_____

_____

_____

_____

Fact File

How old were you when you became a dad?

What was the name of the hospital where I was born?

How long was labour with me?

What time was I born?

How much did I weigh?

Did you take paternity leave? If so, how much?

Fact File

What was my first word?

How old was I when I took my first step?

Beatrix Potter (1866–1943) *The Tale of Peter Rabbit* **(1901)**

'Don't go into Mr McGregor's garden; your father had an accident there, he was put into a pie by Mrs McGregor.'

Being a Dad

Being a dad isn't the easiest job, but it seems to me that you are brilliant at it. I'd really like to know what it feels like to be a father. You are always there for me, at my back, ready to show up whenever I wobble, or to cheer me on during the good times. Maybe knowing how to be a dad is a super-power bestowed on fathers as their baby is born, but I'm pretty sure that's not the case!

This is where I pick your brains about the highs and lows of fatherhood. What are the lessons you've learnt and how has being a father shaped the person you've become? And of course, I want to know when you've been proudest of me, and when you've been most fed up!

....

Can you stick a photograph of the two of us together here?

How do you think being a father has changed you as a person?

_____

_____

_____

_____

_____

_____

_____

What is the hardest thing about being a dad?

_____

_____

_____

_____

_____

_____

_____

What are the funniest moments you remember from when I was growing up?

_____

_____

_____

_____

_____

_____

What was the scariest thing that happened when I was a child?

_____

_____

_____

_____

_____

_____

What are the hobbies or skills you feel you've passed on to me?
Are there things you enjoy that you wish I liked or was good at?

_____

_____

_____

_____

_____

_____

Were there moments when you were particularly proud of me?

_____

_____

_____

_____

_____

_____

When were the times when you were particularly exasperated or
fed up with me?

_____

_____

_____

_____

_____

_____

Is there anything you feel you got wrong as a father? What would
you change if you were to start all over again?

_____

_____

_____

_____

_____

What did you think of my first romantic partner?

_____

_____

_____

_____

_____

How tricky was it combining parenthood with your career?

_____

_____

_____

_____

_____

What do you think is the most important attribute that a father should have?

_____

_____

_____

_____

_____

_____

What top tips would you give to someone who is about to become a dad?

_____

_____

_____

_____

_____

Fact File

What was the worst illness I had as a child?

What was my favourite food when I was little?

Where was our best family holiday from your point of view?

What was my naughtiest moment?

Can you describe my personality as a child in three words?

Can you remember my favourite toy?

Was I a talkative or a quiet child?

Was I a picky eater or adventurous with food?

If you could re-live one day of my childhood, which would it be?

Alexander Pope (1688–1744), *An Essay on Criticism* (1711)

'We think our fathers fools, so wise we grow. Our wiser sons, no doubt will think us so.'

Living Life Now

Being a father is only one part of your identity, and I'd like to know how you feel as you look back over the past and forward to the next stage of your life. This chapter is where I find out how you view your own history, and what your dreams are for the future.

I'm also really interested to find out what you think the most significant changes have been over your lifetime, and what you think the world will look like in another fifty years. What do you think there is to be afraid of or to look forward to?

But it's not just the serious stuff – I'd also like to know about the everyday things. What is your perfect way to spend a Sunday? What is your favourite ice-cream flavour and what would your desert island meal be?

And finally, I'd like to know the one piece of advice you'd like to pass on as a result of all your life experience.

Thank you, Dad!

....

What is the hardest decision you've ever had to make? Would you make it again?

_____

_____

_____

_____

_____

_____

_____

Is there anything you've done that you regret and would do differently now?

_____

_____

_____

_____

_____

Are there hobbies or activities you enjoy at this point in your life that you think I would value if I started to learn them now?

_____

_____

_____

_____

_____

_____

Is there anything you haven't told me about that has happened to you in your life that you can share for the first time now?

_____

_____

_____

_____

_____

What are the most significant events that have happened in your lifetime?

_____

_____

_____

_____

_____

_____

What are the greatest technological and societal changes you have seen in your life so far?

_____

_____

_____

_____

_____

What do you think I have to look forward to in life, and what are the things you most worry about for me in the future?

_____

_____

_____

_____

_____

_____

What are your own dreams for the future? What would you like to do next?

_____

_____

_____

_____

_____

_____

What makes you happy or brings you the most joy?

_____

_____

_____

_____

_____

_____

Can you describe your perfect day?

_____

_____

_____

_____

_____

_____

If you could re-live one particular day in your life, which day would it be?

_____

_____

_____

_____

_____

_____

_____

What is on your bucket list?

_____

_____

_____

_____

_____

_____

If you could re-live your life, are there any important decisions you would change? If so, what are they?

_____

_____

_____

_____

_____

_____

What are the most important practical skills you think I should learn?

_____

_____

_____

_____

_____

_____

Which countries are the ones you'd most like to visit – if money was no object?

_____

_____

_____

_____

_____

_____

Is there something new you feel you'd like to achieve in your life?

_____

_____

_____

_____

_____

_____

Are there any adventures you think you and I should go on together?

_____

_____

_____

_____

_____

_____

What are your hopes for me for the future?

_____

_____

_____

_____

_____

_____

What are you most grateful for?

_____

_____

_____

_____

_____

_____

What do you think was the best thing you did for me, as a father?

_____

_____

_____

_____

_____

_____

What is the advice you would most like me to take forward with me in my life?

_____

_____

_____

_____

_____

_____

Fact File
What is your date of birth?
What is your height?
What is your favourite ice cream flavour?
What would your desert island meal be?

Fact File

What are your top three desert island discs?

What animal would you be?

What is your favourite colour?

Where would you live if you could live anywhere?

Would you rather be famous or rich?

Which sports team would you play for?

Who is your favourite artist?

Milk chocolate or dark chocolate?

Town or country?

Lewis Carroll (1832–1898) *Alice's Adventures in Wonderland* **(1865)**

"'You are old, Father William," the young man said,
    "And your hair has become very white;
And yet you incessantly stand on your head –
    Do you think, at your age, it is right?"'

Can you sketch out a family tree here? Go as far back as you can!

These last few pages are for you to add anything you'd like to say to me that hasn't been covered so far in this journal. Please do add any sketches, poems or photographs that are fun or meaningful to you. Do you have any early stories you might have written? Or perhaps there are some of mine from when I was young that you might have kept that you could reproduce here?

First published in the UK in 2026 by Bedford Square Publishers Ltd,
London, UK

bedfordsquarepublishers.co.uk
@bedsqpublishers

ISBN
978-1-83501-539-1 (Hardback)

2 4 6 8 10 9 7 5 3 1

Typeset in Larken by Palimpsest Book Production Ltd, Falkirk, Stirlingshire

Printed in Great Britain by CPI Group (UK) Ltd, Croydon CR0 4YY

The manufacturer's authorised representative in the EU for
product safety is Easy Access System Europe,
Mustamäe tee 50, 10621 Tallinn, Estonia
gpsr.requests@easproject.com